This book belongs to

All-time Favorite Bible Stories
of the Old Testament

V. Gilbert Beers
Ronald A. Beers

Illustrated by
Daniel J. Hochstatter

Thomas Nelson Publishers, Inc.   Nashville, Tennessee

A Word to Parents

Some Bible stories deserve to be called "All-time Favorites."

That's because they are. These were your favorite Bible stories when you were a child. Perhaps they were your parents' favorite Bible stories when they were children, too. Now they can become favorites for your children.

Why are some stories favorites? These are the stories with unforgettable characters, dramatic events, and wonderful objects. Who could forget Noah, hammering on the great ark for more than a century? And what about Baby Moses, floating in that little papyrus basket in the Nile River? No child should ever grow up without meeting young David as he whirls his sling, ready to conquer the giant Goliath. Joseph is one of our favorites. One day he lies in an Egyptian prison. The next day he rules the land of Egypt. That's because he trusted God to help him.

You'll want your children to stand on the shores of the Red Sea and watch the waters part. You'll want them to see the miracle of manna and the dramatic story of the Golden Calf.

There are great warriors and just plain ordinary people in these stories. You'll want your children to meet them all. Watch while these all-time favorite stories become their all-time favorites, too.

—*V. Gilbert & Ronald A. Beers*

All-time Favorite Bible Stories of the Old Testament

V. Gilbert Beers, Ronald A. Beers

Contents

God Creates a Wonderful World

In the beginning, when God began to create the heavens and earth, the earth had no shape. God's Spirit brooded over these dark vapors. "Let there be light!" God said. Light appeared, and God divided the light from darkness. He called the light "day" and the darkness "night." Thus ended the first day.

"Let the sky and oceans separate," God said. The sky and oceans took form. Thus ended the second day.

"Let the oceans and the dry land separate," God said. God called the dry land "earth" and the oceans "seas." God was pleased. He also caused grass and plants to grow and trees to appear with seeds. This happened on the third day.

On the fourth day God made the sun, moon and stars. The sun shined by day and the moon and stars at night. God was pleased with this work.

God made fish and birds on the fifth day.

On the sixth day He made all kinds of animals, wild animals and cattle. He was pleased with all this, too. On the sixth day God also made a man and a woman. He named the man Adam, and Adam named the woman Eve.

God put the man and woman in a beautiful garden named Eden. They were supposed to take care of the garden and the animals for God. When God finished all He had done, He rested on the seventh day. He was pleased with His work and He was pleased with this special day for rest. God called this day holy for it was the day He rested from all His work.

Adam and Eve Sin

When God put Adam and Eve in the garden of Eden He gave them everything they needed. They could eat every kind of fruit except one. "You must not eat this fruit," God told them. "If you do, you will die."

But Satan came as a snake one day to see Eve. "God is lying," he said. "You will not die if you eat this fruit. Your eyes will be opened and you will know the difference between good and evil."

Of course, God was telling the truth. Satan was lying. God had planned for Adam and Eve to live forever. But if they ate the fruit, they would disobey God. This is sin, and sin does something terrible. It keeps people from living with God forever. That's why God said they would die.

Eve listened to Satan. The fruit looked so good that she ate some. She even gave some to Adam to eat. Suddenly they both realized that they were not wearing clothes. They were ashamed and made aprons of fig leaves to cover themselves.

That evening, Adam and Eve heard God moving through the garden. They were afraid and hid. "Why are you hiding?" God asked.

Then Adam and Eve told God what had happened. So God had to punish them. "You must crawl on your belly in the dust," God told the serpent. "You and the woman's children will fear one another."

"You will have pain and suffering when you have children," God told Eve. Then He told Adam, "You must work hard and sweat to earn your living. When you die, your body will go back into the ground from which I made it."

God also made Adam and Eve leave the garden of Eden. He put mighty angels at the entrance to the garden to keep them out, and a flaming sword to keep them from eating from the Tree of Life. If they ate that fruit, they would live forever, but not the way God wanted them to live.

So the happy days in the garden of Eden were over. That's what happens when we do not obey God, isn't it?

Noah and the Great Flood

As time passed, people sinned more than ever. God saw all this evil and was sorry that He had made these people. At last He said, "I will take these people from the face of the earth, along with their animals."

But Noah was a man who pleased God. So God spoke to Noah and told him what He would do. "I will destroy all other people except you and your family," He said. "You must make a big boat and put each kind of animal and bird on it."

Noah listened carefully and did exactly what God told him. He worked for 120 years to build the big boat. Then he put each kind of animal and bird on it. One day God closed the door of the big boat, the Ark. Then He caused it to rain for 40 days and 40 nights. A great flood of water swept over the earth and all other people and animals were drowned. Only Noah and his family, and the animals and birds on the Ark were saved. Noah and his family lived on this Ark for a long time until the water of the flood disappeared. At last they could open the door and go out on dry land again. When they did, they were the only people on earth. And these were the only animals and birds on earth.

Noah made an altar of stones and burned some meat on it. That was his way of saying "thank you" to God for saving him and his family. Then God put a beautiful rainbow in the sky. It was a special promise from God. "I will never destroy all people and animals with a great flood again," God promised Noah.

The Tower of Babel

Long, long ago everyone on earth spoke the same language. Nobody knows for sure what that language was. But it was not English, or German, or Spanish. It was probably not any other language that people speak today.

More people were being born. Many of them moved to a large plain in the land of Babylon. There they built a great city. In that city they began to build a tower that would reach up to the sky. "This tower will bring us together and make us look powerful and important," the people said. "It will keep us from scattering over the earth." So the people made hundreds of bricks. They made the bricks from mud and baked them in the hot sunlight. Then they began to build the tower.

But God did not like this tower. He did not like what they were trying to do with it. "If they are doing all this now, what will they do later?" God wondered. "I will make them speak different languages. Then they won't understand each other."

God knew that the people who spoke the same language would live together. Those who spoke different languages would move away because they could not understand each other. So that was the way God scattered the people over the earth. The city was not finished. The tower was not finished. The city became known as Babel. The name meant "confusion." Don't you think there must have been a lot of confusion when people began speaking different languages? Don't you think there must have been a lot of confusion when people began moving from Babel?

God Makes a Covenant with Abraham

When Abram was ninety-nine years old, God talked to him one day. "Obey Me and live the way you should," God told Abram. "I will agree to make you into a great nation. You will even be the father of many nations."

Abram fell with his face down in the dust as God talked. "I am changing your name," God told Abram. "I will call you Abraham. This means 'father of nations.'"

"I will keep this agreement through many years," God told Abraham. "I will give all this land to you and your descendants forever. And I will be your God. Your part of the agreement is to obey Me." Then God talked with Abraham about his wife. "Her name is now Sarah," God said. That meant "princess."

God surprised Abraham by telling him that he and Sarah would have a baby boy. Abraham laughed inside when he heard this. "I will have a baby when I am a hundred years old?" he said. "And Sarah will have a baby when she is ninety?"

"You will name him Isaac," God told Abraham. "My agreement will continue through him. He will be born about this time next year." The agreement that God made with Abraham is called a covenant. It was an important promise that would never be broken.

The Destruction of Sodom

After the angels talked with Abraham, they went on their way to Sodom. That evening they arrived at the gate of the city, where Lot was sitting. Lot invited these men to his house and fed them a wonderful meal.

"Get your relatives out of this city," the angels warned Lot. "We will destroy the city and all who are in it because they are so wicked. Hurry!" Lot tried to talk with his daughters' fiances, but they refused to leave. "Then take your wife and daughters and get out of here!" the angels urged.

Lot didn't seem to understand how urgent it was so he didn't hurry. At last the angels grabbed his hand and led Lot and his wife and daughters out of the city.

"Now run for your lives!" they urged. "Run to the mountains and don't look back."

"Please don't send me to the mountains," Lot argued. "Let us go to that little city over there to live." The angels would not argue any more. They let Lot and his family go to the little city, which was called Zoar. The sun was just coming up when Lot and his family reached Zoar. Then God sent fire and flaming sulfur down on Sodom, Gomorrah, and the other cities around them. They were completely destroyed because of their wickedness.

Lot's wife did not obey God, though, for she looked back at Sodom. When she did, she became a pillar of salt.

That morning Abraham looked toward Sodom. He must have felt sad as he saw the smoke rising from the city. But God had kept Lot safe.

Abraham Offers Isaac

The years passed and Isaac grew to be a strong boy. Abraham was proud of his son and loved him very much. But one day God tested Abraham to see if he loved Isaac more than God. "Abraham," God said to him.

"Yes, here I am," Abraham answered.

"Take Isaac, whom you love so very much, and sacrifice him as a burnt offering on a mountain I will show you," God said. Abraham was hurt to hear this, but he would obey God no matter what He asked. So he took wood for the fire and left for the mountain with Isaac and two young servants.

On the third day Abraham and Isaac came to the place that God showed them. This was Mount Moriah. The two servants stayed with the donkey while Isaac carried the wood up the mountain. Abraham carried the knife and the flint to make the fire.

"Where is the lamb for the sacrifice?" Isaac asked.

"God will give it to us," Abraham answered. Abraham built a stone altar on the mountain and placed the wood upon it. Then he tied Isaac and laid him on the wood. But when Abraham lifted the knife, God called to him from heaven. "Put the knife down," God told Abraham. "I know now that you love Me most of all." Then Abraham saw a ram caught by its horns in a bush. So he sacrificed the ram instead of Isaac.

God talked again to Abraham and told him how He would bless him with thousands of descendants.

So Abraham and Isaac went down the mountain. Then they returned home again to Beersheba.

Esau Sells His Birthright

Isaac and Rebekah were very happy together. But they had no children. Many years passed, then at last they had twin sons. The older son was named Esau and the younger son was named Jacob.

As the boys grew up, hairy red-faced Esau became a hunter. Jacob was a quieter young man who liked to help around the home. Thus the father, Isaac, came to like Esau better, while the mother, Rebekah, came to like Jacob better.

One day Jacob was making a pot of lentil stew when Esau came home from hunting. "Give me some of your stew," Esau told Jacob.

"I'll trade you some stew for your birthright," said Jacob.

"When a person is starving, what good is a birthright?" said Esau. "It's a deal!"

"Promise me before God that you mean it," said Jacob.

So Esau promised before God that he was trading his birthright for the stew. A birthright in those days meant the older son got twice as much as any other child. He also became the leader of the family when the father died.

So Jacob gave Esau the stew with bread and Esau ate it. Then he went on with his work as if he had done nothing unusual.

Many years later, Esau would be sorry that he had done this. But it would be too late then to change what had happened.

The Hebrews Become Slaves

When Joseph became governor of Egypt, the Egyptians had plenty of food to eat. But people in other countries did not. So Joseph brought his family to Egypt. He gave them a place to live, land for their herds, and plenty of food.

As time passed, Joseph and his brothers and his father all died. Their children had many children. And these children had many, many children. These people, who became known as Hebrews, filled the land of Goshen. That was the part of Egypt where they lived.

Pharaoh, king of Egypt, began to worry about the Hebrews. He was afraid there would soon be more Hebrews than Egyptians. "If war comes, they may join our enemy," he said. "We must find a way to stop them now."

Pharaoh forced the Hebrews to become slaves. He had cruel taskmasters tell them what to do. They built two cities called Pithom and Rameses.

But the Hebrews kept having more and more children. Being slaves did not keep them from having children.

"Why haven't you obeyed me?" Pharaoh demanded. "Because the Hebrew women have their babies too fast," the nurses answered. "We don't get there in time."

Pharaoh ordered some Hebrew nurses to kill all Hebrew boys as soon as they were born. The girls could live. But the nurses did not obey Pharaoh. They knew God would not be pleased.

The Hebrew people kept on having babies. At last Pharaoh had another plan. He ordered his soldiers to throw all Hebrew baby boys into the Nile River.

Moses Is Born

Two Hebrew slaves, Amram and Jochebed had a new baby boy. But they were afraid that Egyptian soldiers would find him and throw him into the river. Pharaoh, king of Egypt, had ordered his soldiers to kill all the Hebrew baby boys.

Jochebed hid the baby boy at home for three months. But it was getting harder to hide him. She knew someone would find him before long.

One day Jochebed made a little basket. She wove papyrus reeds together. She covered the outside with tar to keep water from getting in. Then she put her baby boy in this basket and set it among the reeds at the edge of the Nile River.

Miriam, the baby's sister, hid by the river. As she watched, Pharaoh's daughter came there to bathe. Suddenly the princess saw the little basket and sent a servant girl to get it. When Pharaoh's daughter opened the basket, she saw the baby boy. He was crying and she felt sorry for him.

"This must be a Hebrew baby," she said.

Miriam came quickly to talk with the princess. "Shall I find a Hebrew woman to take care of the baby for you?" she asked.

"Yes," said the princess.

Miriam ran home and brought her mother to see Pharaoh's daughter. "Take care of the child," she told Jochebed, "and I will pay you."

When the boy was old enough to leave his mother, Jochebed brought him to the princess. The boy became her son and lived in the palace with her. The princess named him "Moses," which meant "draw-out" because she drew him out of the water.

The Burning Bush

Moses became the son of the princess. So he grew up in the palace and was taught to be a prince. He had everything he wanted. But one day Moses got into trouble. He had to run away from Egypt to a land called Midian. He had to live there many years.

Moses became a shepherd in Midian. He married Jethro's daughter Zipporah and took care of Jethro's sheep.

One day Moses was watching the sheep in the desert near Horeb, the mountain of God. Suddenly the angel of the Lord appeared to Moses in a flame of fire in a bush. Moses watched the bush burning, but it never burned up. When he went closer to see what was happening, God spoke to him.

"I want to take your people from their slavery in Egypt," God told Moses. "You will lead them to a good land. I will send you now to Pharaoh. Tell him that he must let these people go."

God showed Moses two signs. When Moses put his shepherd's rod on the ground, it became a serpent. When he picked it up, it became a rod again. That was one sign. When Moses put his hand into his cloak, and took it out, he had leprosy. When he did this again, he was well. That was the other sign.

"I can't speak well," Moses complained.

"I will send your brother Aaron with you," God told Moses. "He is on his way here now to see you."

Moses had no more excuses. So he headed back home to tell Jethro what had happened.

God Sends Plagues to Egypt

God told Moses to go to Egypt and lead the Hebrew slaves to a new land. His brother Aaron would go with him and help him. When Moses and Aaron reached Egypt, they went to see Pharaoh, king of Egypt.

"Let my people go," Moses demanded.

"I will not," said Pharaoh. Then the king made the Hebrew slaves make bricks without straw. That was much harder than making them with straw.

Moses went back to Pharaoh. He told Aaron to throw down his rod and it became a serpent. Surely the king would see this miracle and know that God sent Moses. Then Pharaoh would let the people go.

Pharaoh had his magicians do the same thing. But Aaron's serpent swallowed the others. Still Pharaoh would not let the Hebrew people go.

Moses and Aaron kept coming back to Pharaoh. Each time they did some miracle from God. One time God changed water into blood. He also sent flies, boils, hail, and locusts. One of the worst plagues that God sent was darkness. It lasted three days. The Egyptians were so afraid. But Pharaoh still would not let the Hebrew people go.

At last God sent the worst plague. Every firstborn Egyptian son died, even Pharaoh's oldest son.

At last Pharaoh let the Hebrew people go. That same night they left Egypt. They took their animals and families. They even took gold and silver and jewels which the Egyptians gave them to get them to leave. At last the Hebrew people were free. They were no longer slaves in Egypt.

The Exodus

What a sight! There were thousands and thousands of Hebrews leaving Egypt. God had sent ten terrible plagues upon Egypt. Nine times Pharaoh stubbornly refused to let the Hebrews go. But when all the firstborn sons of Egypt died, Pharaoh told them to leave.

The Egyptian people wanted the Hebrews to leave, too. They gave them gold and silver and jewels and told them to get out of the land. They were afraid they would all die.

The Hebrews left Egypt the same night the firstborn sons of Egypt died. There were six hundred thousand men, plus all the women and children. And there were flocks and herds, and wagons filled with their things.

"This is a day for you to remember," Moses told the people. "The Lord brought you from Egypt with great miracles. Each year at this time, near the end of March, you must remember this special day, which will be called the Passover. When you do, be sure to tell your children why you are celebrating. Remember also when you come into the Promised Land that your firstborn sons belong to the Lord. And your firstborn male animals belong to Him, too."

Crossing the Red Sea

"Take the people along the shore of the Red Sea," God told Moses. "Pharaoh will think you are trapped there and will come after you. Then I will show him that I am the Lord."

Moses did what the Lord said and camped along the shore of the sea. Pharaoh heard about this. Suddenly he changed his mind about the Hebrews and wanted them back as his slaves. Pharaoh got into his chariot and led the best 600 chariots of his entire army after the Hebrews.

The Hebrews were terribly afraid when they saw the army coming. They began to complain to Moses. "You must not be afraid," Moses told the people. "Watch and you will see the wonderful way the Lord will rescue you."

God told Moses to hold out his rod over the sea. Meanwhile the angel of the Lord moved the pillar of cloud between the Egyptian army and the Hebrews, so the Egyptians could not find them. That night it was dark on the Egyptian side of the cloud, but on the Hebrew side there was light.

While this was happening Moses stretched out his rod toward the sea. All night a strong wind blew, and the Lord opened a path through the sea. The water moved aside like great walls, and the bottom of the sea became dry.

The Hebrews walked through the sea on the dry ground. When the Egyptians followed, the Lord caused their chariot wheels to fall off.

When the Hebrews were safe, the Lord told Moses to stretch out the rod again. The sea rushed back and all the Egyptian army was drowned.

The Hebrew people looked at this wonderful miracle and realized what the Lord had done for them. So they trusted the Lord and His helper Moses.

Food in the Wilderness

When God saved the Hebrew people from the Egyptian army, they sang a song. Moses' sister Miriam played a tambourine and sang. Other women followed her, dancing and singing to the Lord, thanking Him for His help.

After that, Moses led the people into the Wilderness of Shur. After three days without water they came to Marah. But the water there was too bitter to drink. The people grumbled again, and said things about Moses that they should not have said. "Must we die? What will we drink?" they complained.

Moses asked God to help. So God showed Moses a tree that would sweeten the water. When Moses threw the tree into the water it was good to drink.

But there was no food in the wilderness so the people complained again. "We had plenty of food in Egypt," they said. "We should have stayed there. We will starve here."

"I will send food," the Lord told Moses. So Moses and Aaron told the people what the Lord said.

That evening quail flew down and covered the camp. Now the people had meat to eat. In the morning there was dew on the ground and when it left the people saw thin white flakes in its place.

"This is the bread the Lord gives you," Moses told them. "Eat it the way He said." Some listened and gathered only enough for one day, as the Lord said. Others tried to gather more, but it rotted and smelled.

Moses was angry because they did not obey. The people called this bread "manna." It was white and tasted like wafers made with honey.

Water from the Rock

When the Israelites left the Wilderness of Sin, they traveled from place to place as the Lord led them. One place was called Rephidim, where there was no water.

The people grew thirsty and quarreled with Moses. "Give us water!" they demanded.

"Why are you complaining to me?" Moses asked. "Why are you testing the Lord?"

But the people were thirsty, so they kept on grumbling and complaining. "Why did you bring us out of Egypt so we would die of thirst here?" they said.

Moses prayed and asked the Lord what to do. "These people are ready to kill me," he said.

"Take some leaders with you," the Lord told Moses. "When you get to the rock at Horeb, hit it and water will come out."

Moses did what the Lord told him, and hit the rock so the leaders could see. Then water came from the rock, as the Lord said it would.

Moses called this place Massah, which meant "testing." That was because the people tested the Lord. He also called it Meribah, which meant "quarreling." That was because the people quarreled about the water.

The Ten Commandments

Moses led the people through the wilderness until they came to Mount Sinai. One day Moses went up into the mountain. The Lord spoke to him there and gave him ten special rules. These rules are so important that we still learn them today and try to do what they say. Here are God's ten important rules:

1. You must not worship any other god than Me.

2. You must not make any idol, or bow down and worship any idol.

3. You must not say My name in a foolish way, or curse with it.

4. You must keep the Sabbath Day holy. Work six days each week and rest on the Sabbath.

5. Honor your father and mother.

6. You must not murder.

7. You must not pretend that another person's husband or wife is your own.

8. You must not steal.

9. You must not lie about someone.

10. You must not want something that belongs to another person.

When Moses came down from the mountain he told the people what God had said. Then there was thunder, lightning, and smoke on Mount Sinai. The people were afraid and begged Moses to speak to them for God. They were afraid they would die if God talked to them.

But Moses told the people not to be afraid of God. They should obey Him and keep His commandments. Then they would have nothing to fear.

The Golden Calf

While Moses was on Mount Sinai, getting the Ten Commandments from the Lord, the people waited below. But it took a long time for the Lord to give Moses all the rules and plans. While Moses was there, the Lord gave him all the plans to make the tabernacle and the things that would go in it.

"We don't know what has happened to Moses," the people said to Aaron, Moses' brother. "Make a god to lead us."

Aaron asked the people for their gold jewelry. He melted the gold and made a golden calf with it. "This is our god," some people said. The next day the people had a big party and danced around the golden calf.

"Go down from Mount Sinai," the Lord told Moses. "Your people have made an idol like a calf. They are bowing before it. Let Me punish them."

But Moses begged the Lord. "Please don't turn against the people and hurt them," he said. "If You do, the Egyptians will say You brought them here to kill them." So the Lord did not hurt the people.

Moses went down from Mount Sinai with the two tablets of stone on which the Ten Commandments were written. When Moses came into the camp where the people were dancing before the golden calf, he was angry. Moses threw down the two tablets and they broke into pieces. Moses ground the golden calf into powder and scattered it on water and made the people drink it.

Moses was angry at Aaron for making the golden calf. But Aaron made an excuse. "I just put the gold into the fire and out came this calf," he said.

The Lord sent a plague because the people had made the golden calf. Many became very sick. That was His punishment for what they had done.

Twelve Spies

"Send spies into the Promised Land, the land of Canaan," the Lord said. Moses sent twelve spies into Canaan to see what it was like.

The spies went into Canaan for forty days. When they came back through the Valley of Eshcol, they cut a large bunch of grapes and brought it with them.

"This land is a good land," the spies said to Moses and the people. "There are wonderful things growing there. But the people are strong. Some are giants. And their cities have tall walls."

Ten spies warned the people not to go into Canaan. "We felt like grasshoppers beside these people," they said.

But two spies, Joshua and Caleb, told the people, "Don't be afraid of these people, for the Lord will help us."

That night the people of Israel cried and said some terrible things about Moses and Aaron. "Let's choose someone to take us back to Egypt," they said. The people even talked about killing Moses and Aaron.

Moses and Aaron were sad. But the Lord told Moses what to say to the people. "Not one of you twenty-one years or older will go into this Promised Land. You must stay in the wilderness for forty years. Your children will go in, but you will not."

So the people had to stay in the wilderness for forty years. Most of them died there because they had not trusted the Lord. They never saw the land God had promised.

Balaam's Donkey

King Balak of Moab was afraid of the Israelites. They had already defeated his neighbors, the Amorites. Now they were camped near his land.

The Moabites asked another neighbor, the Midianites, to help. But they were still not strong enough to fight the people of Israel. So they sent messengers to a prophet named Balaam, asking him to come and curse the people of Israel. They thought this would hurt the Israelites.

"Stay here tonight," Balaam told the messengers. "I will ask the Lord what to do." When he did, the Lord told him not to go with the men.

King Balak sent more important messengers the next time. And he sent more of them. Balaam must have begged the Lord until He let him go, for the Lord did not really want him to do it. When the Lord saw Balaam ride on his donkey with the men, He was angry.

Then the Angel of the Lord stood in the road in front of the donkey. The donkey saw the angel but Balaam did not. So the donkey ran off the road into a field.

Balaam beat his donkey and got her back on the road. But this time the donkey squeezed close to a wall to stay away from the angel. Balaam's foot was hurt, so Balaam beat the donkey again.

Now the angel moved ahead at a place where the donkey could not pass. This time the donkey lay down on the road. Balaam beat her again. Suddenly the donkey began to talk. Then the Lord let Balaam see what the donkey had seen.

"Go with these men, but say only what I tell you," the angel said.

Balaam went with the men. Then he told King Balak, "I will say only what the Lord tells me to say." And he did. Balaam would not curse the people of Israel, for the Lord told him not to do it.

Samuel Is Born

In the days when the Judges ruled Israel, there was a man named Elkanah who had two wives. In those days some men married more than one wife. But as you will see, this usually brought trouble.

Peninnah, one of Elkanah's wives, had children. That was a great honor in Israel at that time. Peninnah made fun of the other wife, Hannah, who had no children. Poor Hannah was so sad and ashamed that she often cried.

Each year Elkanah went to Shiloh with his family to worship at the tabernacle, God's house. Each year Peninnah made fun of Hannah.

After dinner one evening Hannah went to the tabernacle and began to pray to the Lord. "Give me a son, and I will give him back to You," Hannah prayed.

Eli the priest, the man in charge of the tabernacle, saw her. He saw her moving her lips but didn't hear her praying, so he thought she was drunk. "Why do you come to God's house drunk?" he demanded. "Stop doing that!"

"But I haven't been drinking," said Hannah. "I am praying that God will give me something special."

"Then may He do it," said Eli.

Hannah was happy to hear Eli say that. Now she was sure God would give her a son. Some time later Hannah did have a baby boy. She named him Samuel, which meant "asked God" because as she said, "I asked God to give me this boy."

Of course Hannah was very happy with her new son. And she remembered her promise. to give him to God.

God Speaks to Samuel

When Samuel was still a little boy, his mother Hannah gave him to the Lord. She brought him to the tabernacle, God's house. Samuel became God's helper, and a helper for old Eli, the priest, the man in charge of the tabernacle.

God did not speak often to people in those days, so what happened one night to the boy Samuel was quite unusual. This is the way it happened. Eli, old and blind now, had gone to bed. So had Samuel, who slept in the holy inner room of the tabernacle where the Ark of the Covenant was kept. Suddenly God called to Samuel.

"Samuel! Samuel!" He said. Samuel thought Eli had called, so he ran to see what he wanted.

"Go back to bed," Eli said. "I did not call you." This happened three times.

"If God calls you again, say that you are listening," Eli told Samuel.

When Samuel went back to bed, God did call again. "I'm listening," Samuel said to God. Then God told Samuel what He was going to do to Eli and his sons.

"I will punish them all," He said. "I have warned them about this."

Samuel stayed in bed all night. In the morning he opened the tabernacle doors as he always did. He was afraid to tell Eli what God had said. "You must tell me all that God said to you," Eli told Samuel. So Samuel told Eli what God had said. "God must do what He thinks is best," said Eli.

As the boy Samuel grew to be a man, people could see that God was with him. So they listened to Samuel. They knew that he would be God's prophet. God did give Samuel more messages. And Samuel told the people what God said.

Saul Is Made King

Samuel became a great judge, a ruler over Israel. He was a good one, too, for he went from place to place, helping people know what God wanted them to do.

Samuel grew old and could not do his work any more. So he retired and made his sons judges in his place. His oldest sons, Joel and Abijah, ruled at Beersheba. But they were greedy men and took bribes. At last the leaders of Israel had enough of this. They went to Samuel and demanded, "We want a king like the other nations around us." Samuel was upset and talked to the Lord about this.

"Warn them that a king will demand much from them," the Lord said. But the people still wanted a king. Then the Lord pointed out to Samuel that Saul, the son of a wealthy man named Kish, would be king. Samuel took some olive oil and poured it over Saul's head. That was called anointing. It showed Saul and others that Saul would be king.

Saul was a tall man. Most people just reached up to his shoulders. When Samuel brought the people together and told them Saul would be their king, the people shouted, "Long live the king." Samuel told the people what they must do. He wrote in a book what the king should do and put it in a special place before the Lord. Not all of the people were happy with their new king.

Some troublemakers said, "How can this man save us?" They did not even bring their new king a present, as the others did. But Saul refused to let this bother him.

Jonathan's Bravery

King Saul had only 600 trembling men left. The Philistines had thousands, with horses, and chariots, and swords. Saul's men did not even have swords.

One day Saul's son Jonathan headed toward the Philistine camp with his bodyguard. They had to climb up the steep wall of a ravine to get there.

"If the Philistines tell us to stay where we are, that will be God's way of telling us not to fight," said Jonathan. "But if they tell us to come up and fight, that will be God's way of telling us to go and fight."

When the Philistines saw Jonathan, they told him to come up and fight. So, Jonathan and his bodyguard climbed up the steep wall to the Philistine army camp. Suddenly the Philistines began to fight each other. Saul and his 600 men joined the battle, along with the men who had run away from Saul's army.

The Philistines began running from Saul's men. Then Saul made a foolish vow. "A curse on anyone who eats before evening," he said.

Jonathan did not hear what Saul said. So when they went through a forest, he dipped a stick into a honeycomb and ate some honey. When evening came Saul asked the Lord if they should keep going after the Philistines. But the Lord would not answer.

"We must find out what sin was done today," Saul said. "Whoever has sinned must die." Saul found then that Jonathan had eaten some honey. "You must die for this," he said. But the soldiers of Israel would not let that happen.

"Jonathan saved Israel today," they said. "He must not die." So they would not let Saul execute Jonathan.

Samuel Anoints David

Saul was a good military man, leading his army to some great victories. But he was not the kind of king God wanted. Saul did not like to obey God. Of course even a king needs to obey God. Samuel was sorry to see this happen.

"You have felt sorry long enough," God told Samuel one day. "Go to Bethlehem. I have chosen a son of Jesse to be the next king."

"Saul will kill me if he hears what I am doing," said Samuel.

"Take a heifer and make an offering there," God said. "When you do, I will show you which son is to be king. Then you can pour olive oil on him to anoint him." Samuel did exactly what God said. He always tried to do that.

Jesse's first son, Eliab, was tall and handsome. "This must be the one," Samuel thought.

"No he isn't," God said. "You must not judge by how tall or handsome a man is. I don't look at others that way. I look at their heart."

Jesse brought each of his seven sons to Samuel. "God has not chosen any of these to be the next king," Samuel told Jesse. "Do you have any other sons?"

"The youngest is out in the fields watching the sheep," said Jesse.

"Bring him here now," Samuel said. "We will not eat until he has come." Jesse brought David, a good looking young man with the well-tanned face of an outdoorsman.

"This is the one I have chosen," God told Samuel. "Anoint him."

So Samuel poured a little horn of olive oil on David's head while his brothers watched. Then God's Spirit came upon David and gave him great power.

David and Goliath

The Philistines gathered their soldiers for a great battle between Socoh and Azekah. Saul gathered his Israelite army at the Valley of Elah. The Philistines were on one side of the valley and the Israelites on the other side.

One day a Philistine giant named Goliath came out into the valley. He was over nine feet tall, with a bronze helmet, a 200 pound armored suit, and bronze leg coverings. He carried a bronze javelin with a 25 pound iron head. His armor bearer carried a large shield for him.

Goliath shouted to the Israelites. "Send a man to fight me. If your soldier kills me, you win the battle. If I kill him, we win the battle." Saul and his soldiers were afraid. They heard Goliath shout this every day for 40 days, twice each day.

One day Jesse sent his son David to the army camp with food for his brothers—Eliab, Abinadab, and Shammah, who served in Saul's army. He heard Goliath shouting and it made him angry. "I'll go fight this Philistine!" said David.

"All right, do it," said King Saul. "May God be with you." At first, Saul put his armor on David. But David could not fight with that. So he took five smooth stones from the brook and put them in his shepherd's bag. Then with his shepherd's staff and sling, he went to fight Goliath.

Goliath was angry that this young man came to fight this way. But David said, "I come to fight in the name of the Lord. He will conquer you."

As Goliath rushed toward him, David whipped a stone at Goliath with his sling. The stone sank into the giant's forehead and he fell dead to the ground.

David grabbed Goliath's sword and cut off his head. When the Philistine soldiers saw that they ran. The Israelites chased them and won a great battle.

The Friendship of David and Jonathan

Jonathan, son of King Saul, had watched as David went out to fight the Philistine giant Goliath. No other man would do this, and David was not even a soldier in Saul's army.

When David was brought to Saul, Jonathan admired him greatly. The two became close friends, and developed a strong bond of love that day. Jonathan swore that he would be like a brother to David. To show that he really meant this, he gave David his robe, his sword, his bow, and his belt.

King Saul decided to keep David at the palace instead of letting him go home to Bethlehem. He made David his army commander and his special assistant at the palace. The soldiers were delighted that David would lead them.

But something strange happened the day David killed Goliath. On the way home some women came out singing and dancing with tambourines and cymbals. They sang about David killing ten thousands and Saul killing only thousands. This made Saul jealous, for it gave more honor to David than to Saul.

"I suppose they will now try to make him king," Saul grumbled. So he began to watch David carefully.

Saul Tries to Kill David

King Saul was jealous. After David killed Goliath, some women sang songs about David killing tens of thousands while Saul killed only thousands. Saul wondered if the people would try to make David king instead of him.

The next day Saul had a temper tantrum. David played the harp for him, as he often did, to soothe him. Saul kept on playing with his spear while David did this. Then suddenly Saul threw the spear at David, hoping to pin him to the wall and kill him. David jumped aside. This same thing happened another time. Saul became so jealous that he demoted David to captain. But this only made David more popular. As David kept on succeeding in all he did, Saul became even more jealous.

Saul offered to let David marry his oldest daughter Merab. But then he had her marry a man named Adriel instead. Then another of Saul's daughters, Michal, fell in love with David. Saul offered to let David marry her. "All you need to do is kill 100 Philistines," Saul told David. So David and his men killed 200. Then David and Michal were married.

When David became more popular than ever, Saul tried to get Jonathan and some others to kill him. But they wouldn't.

"David has always tried to help you," Jonathan told Saul. "So why should you try to kill him now?" For awhile Saul did not try to kill David. But one day when Saul was listening to David play the harp, he threw his spear at him and almost killed him. Then he ordered his men to kill David when he left his house in the morning. But Michal learned of it and helped David escape during the night.

Jonathan Warns David

"Why does your father want to kill me?" David asked his friend Jonathan.

"But he doesn't," said Jonathan. He did not realize how much King Saul, his father, wanted to kill David.

"Your father would not tell you that he wants to kill me," said David. "He knows we are good friends."

"But what can I do?" Jonathan asked.

"Tomorrow starts the three-day feast of the New Moon," said David. "I won't be there. If Saul is angry, tell me and we will know he wants to kill me."

So Jonathan and David planned a signal. The next day David would hide by a pile of rocks. Jonathan would shoot three arrows nearby. Jonathan would send a boy after the arrows. If he told the boy that the arrows were on this side of him, David would know all was well. But if he said the arrows were on the other side of him, he would know Saul wanted to kill him.

On the third day of the feast Saul asked Jonathan about David. Jonathan gave an excuse that he and David had planned. Saul was so angry that he tried to kill Jonathan. Then Jonathan knew for sure that Saul wanted to kill David.

The next morning Jonathan shot the three arrows. When the boy ran for them, Jonathan called out, "They are on the other side of you." That was the signal that Saul really did want to kill David.

When Jonathan sent the boy back to town with his bow and arrows, David came from his hiding place. The two friends shook hands and cried.

"Let's remember what we have promised," Jonathan told David. They were such good friends they had promised to be kind to one another and to one another's children as long as they lived. So David left and Jonathan went back to town.

Saul Dies in Battle

One day the Israelites and Philistines fought on Mount Gilboa. Many Israelites were killed. The rest ran away. Even King Saul and his sons tried to run away. But the Philistines caught them. They killed Saul's sons—Jonathan, Abinidab, and Malchishua.

The Philistine archers went after King Saul. They wounded him with their arrows.

"Kill me!" Saul told his armor bearer. "If you don't, they will torture me."

The armor bearer was afraid to kill his king. So Saul fell on his own sword and died. The armor bearer also fell on his sword and died.

The Israelites east of the Jordan River heard what had happened. They were afraid and ran away. Then the Philistines came and lived in their towns.

The next day the Philistines went to the battlefield to take things from the dead Israelites. When they found Saul and his sons, they cut off Saul's head. They took his armor, and sent word throughout the land that King Saul was dead.

The Philistines hung Saul's weapons in the temple of the goddess Ashtaroth. They hung his body on the wall of Beth-shan.

But brave Israelite warriors from Jabesh-gilead marched all night. They took the bodies of Saul and his sons back home and burned them there. Later they buried their bones under the large tamarisk tree in town Then they fasted for seven days.

David Becomes King

After Saul died, David asked the Lord if he should go home to Judah. When the Lord said yes, David asked where he should go.

"To Hebron," the Lord told David.

David moved to Hebron, not far from his boyhood home at Bethlehem. He took with him his two wives Ahinoam and Abigail. Some of David's friends also came with their families.

One day the leaders of Judah came to Hebron and made David their king. They anointed him, pouring olive oil on his head. This was the way leaders showed that the Lord was making someone king.

David was pleased that the people of Jabesh-gilead had buried Saul. He sent them a message. "The Lord will bless you and I will be kind to you because you did this," David told them. "Now that Saul is dead, the leaders of Judah have made me their king. I hope you will make me your king too."

But it would not be that easy. Abner, commander of Saul's army, had taken Saul's son Ishbosheth to Mahanaim. The people there made him king over the rest of Israel. He was forty, and ruled for two years. David ruled over Judah for seven and one half years.

Absalom Rebels Against David

David's handsome son Absalom decided that he wanted to be king. He would rebel against his father and become king of Israel. But first he must win many of Israel's leaders to him.

This is the way he did it. Absalom got a chariot and horses and rode to the city gate each day. People came with their complaints and Absalom listened to them. "If I were king, I would do more for you," he would say. Many began to wish he was king instead of David. Before long many leaders were ready to make him king.

One day Absalom went with some leaders to Hebron. He had them make him king.

David and his trusted men ran away when they heard this. David would not fight his son. When David was gone, Absalom moved into his palace in Jerusalem. He made plans to kill his father so no one would keep him from being king.

Absalom had two advisors. Ahithophel was loyal to him. But Hushai was secretly loyal to King David. Hushai gave advice which seemed good but would hurt Absalom.

One day Hushai advised Absalom to lead an army against David. Absalom listened to Hushai. But he did not know that Hushai had sent word to David to prepare his soldiers for this battle. Absalom's men were defeated and Absalom was killed. The plot to kill David had failed.

David Plans the Temple

King David wanted to build a temple for the Lord. It would be at the threshing floor which he bought from Araunah. But the Lord would not let him do it. David had been a man of war and had killed too many people. "Solomon your son will build My temple," the Lord told David.

While David was still king, he made plans for the temple. He gathered much of the building material. He had almost 4,000 tons of gold and 40,000 tons of silver. He also had jewels, bronze, iron, wood, and stones. David found workmen to build the temple and take care of it.

David called the leaders of his people together. He told them that Solomon would build the temple, as the Lord commanded.

"Serve the Lord," David told his son Solomon. "Build His temple. If you are with the Lord, He will be with you. If you turn against Him, He will turn against you."

Before all the people, David praised the Lord. "Praise the Lord," the people answered.

Solomon was made king and Zadok anointed him. The whole nation respected Solomon and promised to be loyal to him.

Solomon's Wisdom

Solomon ruled wisely and the Lord was with him. One day he took officials and leaders with him to Gibeon. There he gave a thousand burnt offerings at the tabernacle.

That night the Lord appeared to Solomon in a dream and promised to give whatever he asked. "Give me wisdom to rule my people justly," said Solomon.

The Lord was pleased with Solomon's choice. "You will have wisdom," He promised. "Since you did not ask for money and honor, I will give those to you too."

Later Solomon showed how wise he was. Two women brought a baby to him. "It's my baby," said the first woman. "We live together. The other night this woman rolled over on her baby and smothered it. She put her dead baby beside me and my baby beside her."

"No, it's my baby," said the second woman. Then the women began to argue.

"Bring a sword," said Solomon. When someone brought a sword, Solomon ordered the baby cut in two. "Give half to each woman," he said.

"No!" said the first woman. "Don't do that! Let her have the baby."

"Cut the baby in two," said the other woman.

"Give the baby to the first woman," said Solomon. "She is the real mother."

The people had great respect for Solomon when they heard about this. They knew the Lord had made him wise.

Solomon Builds the Temple

King Solomon sent messengers to King Hiram of Tyre. "You were my father's friend," he said. "You sold cedar logs for his palace. Please work with me as I build the temple."

Hiram was glad to sell cedar logs to Solomon. He also sent Huram, a wise master craftsman. Huram helped Solomon build the temple.

Solomon built the temple on Mount Moriah. King David had bought Araunah's threshing floor there. The temple was 90 feet long and 30 feet wide, with two large bronze columns at the entrance.

Solomon built a large bronze altar and a large bronze tank where the priests could wash. He built ten basins where the animal meat for offerings could be washed. He made golden lampstands, golden bowls, and many beautiful pieces of equipment to use for the offerings. At last the Ark of the Covenant, the golden box with the Ten Commandments inside, was put in the Most Holy Place.

When the temple was finished, Solomon prayed before the people who gathered there. "Listen to our prayers and bless us," Solomon prayed.

Fire came from heaven and burned the meat on the altar. In a dazzling light, the Lord came into the temple. When the people saw this, they fell down and worshiped the Lord. After a great feast, the people went home, happy that the Lord was blessing them.

The Kingdom Divides

When Solomon died, his son Rehoboam went to Shechem. He wanted the ten northern tribes of Israel to make him king.

Jeroboam heard of Solomon's death and came home from Egypt. He and other leaders of Israel went to see Rehoboam. "Treat us better than your father Solomon did and we will be loyal to you," they said.

"Come back in three days and I will give you an answer," said Rehoboam.

Rehoboam talked with his older advisors. "Treat these people kindly," they said. "If you do, they will serve you."

Then Rehoboam talked to his younger advisors. "Tell them you will not be as kind as your father Solomon," said the younger men. So that is what Rehoboam said.

The leaders of the ten tribes of Israel rebelled against Rehoboam. They killed Adoniram, Rehoboam's man in charge of forced labor. Rehoboam got into his chariot and escaped to Jerusalem.

Then the leaders of Israel made Jeroboam king of their ten tribes. Rehoboam was king over the tribe of Judah, where Jerusalem was located.

Now there were two kingdoms. The Northern Kingdom, Israel, had ten tribes. Jeroboam was its king. The Southern Kingdom, Judah, had one tribe and the city of Jerusalem. Rehoboam was its king.